D0931093

Theory of Religion

Paul Nelson Gumbel
Columbia University '92
—for Rare Columbian w/
E. Pagtory

Translated by Robert Hurley

Theory of Religion

Georges Bataille

ZONE BOOKS · NEW YORK

1989

ZONE BOOKS
611 Broadway Suite 838
New York, NY 10012

Originally published in France as *Théorie de la Religion*
© 1973 by Éditions Gallimard.

Printed in the United States of America

Distributed by The MIT Press,
Cambridge, Massachusetts, and London, England

Library of Congress Cataloging-in-Publication Data

Bataille, Georges, 1897–1962.
    Theory of religion.

    Translation of: Théorie de la religion.
    Bibliography: p.
    1. Religion. I. Title.
BL48.B3713 1989 200'.1   88-20591
ISBN 0-942299-08-6 (alk. paper)
ISBN 0-942299-09-4 (pbk.: alk. paper)

Desire is what transforms Being, revealed to itself by itself in (true) knowledge, into an "object" revealed to a "subject" different from the object and "opposed" to it. It is in and by — or better still, as — "his" Desire that man is formed and is revealed — to himself and to others — as an I, as the I that is essentially different from, and radically opposed to, the non-I. The (human) I is the I of a Desire or of Desire.

The very being of man, the self-conscious being, therefore, implies and presupposes Desire. Consequently, the human reality can be formed and maintained only within a biological reality, an animal life. But, if animal Desire is the necessary condition of self-consciousness, it is not the sufficient condition. By itself, this Desire constitutes only the Sentiment of self.

In contrast to the knowledge that keeps man in a passive quietude, Desire dis-quiets him and moves him to action. Born of Desire, action tends to satisfy it, and can do so only by the "negation," the destruction, or at least the transformation, of the desired object: to satisfy hunger, for example, the food must be destroyed or, in any case, transformed. Thus, all action is "negating."

— Alexandre Kojève
Introduction to the Reading of Hegel

Contents

Where This Book Is Situated

The foundation of one's thought is the thought of another; thought is like a brick cemented into a wall. It is a simulacrum of thought if, in his looking back on himself, the being who thinks sees a free brick and not the price this semblance of freedom costs him: he doesn't see the waste ground and the heaps of detritus to which a sensitive vanity consigns him with his brick.

The work of the mason, who assembles, is the work that matters. Thus the adjoining bricks, in a book, should not be less visible than the new brick, which is the book. What is offered the reader, in fact, cannot be an element, but must be the ensemble in which it is inserted: it is the whole human assemblage and edifice, which must be, not just a pile of scraps, but rather a self-consciousness.

In a sense the unlimited assemblage is the impossible. It takes courage and stubbornness not to go slack. Everything invites one to drop the substance for the shadow, to forsake the open and impersonal movement of thought for the isolated opinion. Of course the isolated opinion is also the shortest means of revealing what the assemblage essentially is – the impossible. But it has this deep meaning only if it is not conscious of the fact.

This powerlessness defines an apex of possibility, or at least, awareness of the impossibility opens consciousness to all that is possible for it to think. In this gathering place, where violence is rife, at the boundary of that which escapes cohesion, he who reflects within cohesion realizes that there is no longer any room for him.

Introduction

This "theory of religion" outlines what a finished work would be: I have tried to express a *mobile* thought, without seeking its definitive state.

A philosophy is a coherent sum or it is nothing, but it expresses the individual, not indissoluble mankind. It must therefore remain open to the developments that will follow, in human thought . . . where those who think, insofar as they reject their otherness (that which they are not) are already lost in the universal oblivion. A philosophy is never a house; it is a construction site. But its incompletion is not that of science. Science draws up a multitude of finished parts and only its whole presents empty spaces, whereas in our striving for cohesiveness, the incompletion is not restricted to the lacunae of thought; at every point, at each point, there is the impossibility of the final state.

This condition of impossibility is not the excuse for

undeniable deficiencies; it limits all real philosophy. The scientist is he who *agrees* to wait. The philosopher himself waits, but he cannot do so legitimately. Philosophy responds from the start to an irresolvable exigency. No one can "be" independently of a response to the question that it raises. Thus the philosopher's response is necessarily given before the elaboration of a philosophy and if it changes in the elaboration, sometimes even owing to the results obtained, *it cannot justifiably be subordinated to them.* Philosophy's response cannot be an effect of philosophical labors, and while it may not be arbitrary, this assumes, given from the start, a contempt for the individual position and an extreme mobility of thought, open to all previous or *subsequent* movements; and, linked to the response from the start, or rather, consubstantial with the response, the dissatisfaction and incompleteness of thought.

So it is an act of consciousness, while carrying one's elucidation to the limit of immediate possibilities, not to seek a definitive state that will never be granted. Doubtless it is necessary to bring one's thinking, which moves within domains already explored, up to the level of formulated knowledge. And in any case the response itself is *in fact* meaningless unless it is that of an intellectually developed individual. But if the second of these conditions must be satisfied beforehand, no one can meet the first except approximately: unless one limited the movement of thought to restricted domains, as scientists do, no one could assimilate the acquired knowledge. To the essential incompletion of thought this adds an inevitable *de facto* incompletion. Moreover, rigor demands a clear recognition of these conditions.

These principles are far removed from a way of philosophizing that is currently receiving if not the acceptance at least the curiosity of the public. Even if they are strongly opposed to the modern insistence that attaches to the individual and the individual's isolation. There cannot be any philosophy of the individual and the exercise of thought cannot have any other outcome than the negation of individual perspectives. A basic problem is linked to the very idea of philosophy: how to get out of the human situation. How to shift from a reflection subordinated to necessary action, condemned to useful distinction, to self-consciousness as consciousness of the being without essence – but conscious?

The inevitable incompletion does not in any way delay the response, which is a movement – were it in a sense the lack of a response. On the contrary, it gives it the truth of the impossible, the truth of a scream. The basic paradox of this "theory of religion," which posits the individual as a "thing," and a negation of intimacy, brings a powerlessness to light, no doubt, but the cry of this powerlessness is a prelude to the deepest silence.

PART ONE

The Basic Data

Chapter I

Animality

Immanence of the Eater and the Eaten

I consider animality from a narrow viewpoint that seems questionable to me, but its value will become clear in the course of the exposition. From this viewpoint, animality is immediacy or immanence.

The immanence of the animal with respect to its milieu is given in a precise situation, the importance of which is fundamental. I will not speak of it continually, but will not be able to lose sight of it; the very conclusion of my statements will return to this starting point: *the situation is given when one animal eats another.*

What is given when one animal eats another is always the *fellow creature* of the one that eats. It is in this sense that I speak of immanence.

I do not mean a *fellow creature* perceived as such, but there is no transcendence between the eater and the eaten; there is a difference, of course, but this animal that eats

17

the other cannot confront it in an affirmation of that difference.

Animals of a given species do not eat one another. . . . Perhaps, but this does not matter if the goshawk eating the hen does not distinguish it clearly from itself, in the same way that we distinguish an object from ourselves. The distinction requires a positing of the object as such. There does not exist any *discernible* difference if the object has not been posited. The animal that another animal eats is not yet given as an object. Between the animal that is eaten and the one that eats, there is no relation of *subordination* like that connecting an object, a thing, to man, who refuses to be viewed as a thing. For the animal, nothing is given through time. It is insofar as we are human that the object exists in time where its duration is perceptible. But the animal eaten by another exists this side of duration; it is consumed, destroyed, and this is only a disappearance in a world where nothing is posited beyond the present.

There is nothing in animal life that introduces the relation of the master to the one he commands, nothing that might establish autonomy on one side and dependence on the other. Animals, since they eat one another, are of unequal strength, but there is never anything between them except that quantitative difference. The lion is not the king of the beasts: in the movement of the waters he is only a higher wave overturning the other, weaker ones.

That one animal eats another scarcely alters a fundamental situation: every animal is *in the world like water in water*. The animal situation does contain a component of the human situation; if need be, the animal can be regarded as a subject for which the rest of the world is an object, but it is never given the possibility of regarding itself in this way. Elements of this situation can be grasped by human intelligence, but the animal cannot *realize* them.

Dependence and Independence of the Animal

It is true that the animal, like the plant, has no autonomy in relation to the rest of the world. An atom of nitrogen, of gold, or a molecule of water exist without needing anything from what surrounds them; they remain in a state of perfect immanence: there is never a necessity, and more generally nothing ever matters in the immanent relation of one atom to another or to others. The immanence of a living organism in the world is very different: an organism seeks elements around it (or outside it) which are immanent to it and with which it must establish (relatively stabilize) relations of immanence. Already it is no longer like water in water. Or if it is, this is only provided it manages to *nourish* itself. If it does not, it suf-

19

fers and dies: the flow (the immanence) from outside to inside, from inside to outside, which is organic life, only lasts under certain conditions.

An organism, moreover, is separated from processes that are similar to it; each organism is detached from other organisms: in this sense organic life, at the same time that it accentuates the relation with the world, withdraws from the world, isolates the plant or the animal which can theoretically be regarded as autonomous worlds, so long as the fundamental relation of nutrition is left aside.

The Poetic Fallacy of Animality

Nothing, as a matter of fact, is more closed to us than this animal life from which we are descended. Nothing is more foreign to our way of thinking than the earth in the middle of the silent universe and having neither the meaning that man gives things, nor the meaninglessness of things as soon as we try to imagine them without a consciousness that reflects them. In reality, we can never imagine things without consciousness except arbitrarily, since *we* and *imagine* imply consciousness, our consciousness, adhering indelibly to their presence. We can doubtless tell ourselves that this adhesion is fragile, in that we will cease to *be there,* one day even for good. But the appearance of a thing is never conceivable except in a consciousness taking the place of my consciousness, if mine has disappeared. This is a simple truth, but animal life, halfway distant from *our* consciousness, presents us with a more disconcerting enigma. In picturing the universe without man, a universe in which only the animal's gaze would be opened to things, the animal being neither a thing nor a man, we can only call up a vision in which we see *nothing,* since the object of this vision is a movement that glides from things that have no meaning by themselves to the world full of meaning implied by man giving each thing his own. This is why we cannot describe such an object in a precise way. Or rather, the correct way to speak of it can *overtly* only be poetic, in that poetry describes nothing that does not slip toward the unknowable. Just as we can speak fictively of the past as if it were a present, we speak finally of prehistoric animals, as well as plants, rocks, and bodies of water, *as if* they were things, but to describe a landscape tied to these conditions is only nonsense, or a poetic leap. There was no landscape in a world where the eyes that opened did not apprehend what they looked at, where indeed, in our terms, the eyes did not see. And if, now, in my mind's confusion, *stupidly* contemplating that absence of vision, I begin to say: "There was no vision, there was nothing – nothing but an empty intoxication limited by terror, suffering, and death, which gave it a kind of thickness . . ."

I am only abusing a poetic capacity, substituting a vague fulguration for the nothing of ignorance. I know: the mind cannot dispense with a fulguration of words that makes a fascinating halo for it: that is its richness, its glory, and a sign of sovereignty. But this poetry is only a way by which a man goes from a world full of meaning to the final dislocation of meanings, of all meaning, which soon proves to be unavoidable. There is only one difference between the absurdity of things envisaged without man's gaze and that of things among which the animal is present; it is that the former absurdity immediately suggests to us the apparent reduction of the exact sciences, whereas the latter hands us over to the sticky temptation of poetry, for, not being simply a thing, the animal is not closed and inscrutable to us. The animal opens before me a depth that attracts me and is familiar to me. In a sense, I know this depth: it is my own. It is also that which is farthest removed from me, that which deserves the name depth, which means precisely *that which is unfathomable to me.* But this too is poetry. . . . Insofar as I can *also* see the animal as a thing (if I eat it – in my own way, which is not that of another animal – or if I enslave it or treat it as an object of science), its absurdity is just as direct (if one prefers, just as near) as that of stones or air, but it is not always, and never entirely, reducible to that kind of inferior reality which we attribute to things. Something tender, secret, and painful draws out the intimacy which keeps vigil in us, extending its glimmer into that animal darkness. In the end, all that I can maintain is that such a view, which plunges me into the night and dazzles me, brings me close to the moment when – I will no longer doubt this – the distinct clarity of consciousness will move me farthest away, finally, from that unknowable truth which, from myself to the world, appears to me only to slip away.

The Animal Is in the World like Water in Water

I will speak of that unknowable later. For the moment, I need to set apart from the dazzle of poetry that which, from the standpoint of experience, appears distinctly and clearly.

I am able to say that the animal world is that of immanence and immediacy, for that world, which is closed to us, is so to the extent that we cannot discern in it an ability to transcend itself. Such a truth is negative, and we will not be able to establish it absolutely. We can at least imagine an embryo of that ability in animals, but we cannot discern it clearly enough. While a study of those embryonic aptitudes can be done, such a study will not yield any perspectives that invalidate our view of immanent animality, which will remain unavoidable *for us.* It is only within the limits of

23

the human that the transcendence of things in relation to consciousness (or of consciousness in relation to things) is manifested. Indeed transcendence is nothing if it is not embryonic, if it is not constituted as solids are, which is to say, immutably, under certain given conditions. In reality, we are incapable of basing ourselves on unstable coagulations and we must confine ourselves to regarding animality, from the outside, in the light of an absence of transcendence. Unavoidably, in our eyes, the animal is in the world like water in water.

The animal has diverse behaviors according to diverse situations. These behaviors are the starting points for possible distinctions, but distinguishing would demand the transcendence of the object having become distinct. The diversity of animal behaviors does not establish any conscious distinction among the diverse situations. The animals which do not eat a fellow creature of the same species still do not have the ability to recognize it as such, so that a new situation, in which the normal behavior is not triggered, may suffice to remove an obstacle without there being an awareness of its having been removed. We cannot say concerning a wolf which eats another wolf that it violates the law decreeing that ordinarily *wolves do not eat one another.* It does not violate this law; it has simply found itself in circumstances where the law no longer applies. In spite of this, there is, for the wolf, a continuity between itself and the world. Attractive or distressing phenomena arise before it; other phenomena do not correspond either to individuals of the same species, to food, or to anything attractive or repellent, so that what appears has no meaning, or is a sign of something else. Nothing breaks a continuity in which fear itself does not announce anything that might be distinguished before being dead. Even the fighting between rivals is another convulsion where insubstantial shadows emerge from the inevitable responses to stimuli. If the animal that has brought down its rival does not apprehend the other's death as does a man behaving triumphantly, this is because its rival had not broken a continuity that the rival's death does not reestablish. This continuity was not called into question, but rather the identity of desires of two beings set one against the other in mortal combat. The apathy that the gaze of the animal expresses after the combat is the sign of an existence that is essentially on a level with the world in which it moves like water in water.

Humanity and the Development

of the Profane World

For the moment, I will not try to give the foregoing a firmer support. What I have said implies an excursion of the intellect outside the domain of the discontinuous which is at least its privileged domain. I wish to pass without further delay to that solid milieu on which we think we can rely.

The Positing of the Object: The Tool
The positing of the object, which is not given in animality, is in the human use of tools; that is, if the tools as middle terms are adapted to the intended result – if their users perfect them. Insofar as tools are developed with their end in view, consciousness posits them as objects, as interruptions in the indistinct continuity. The developed tool is the nascent form of the non-I.

The tool brings exteriority into a world where the

27

subject has a part in the elements it distinguishes, where it has a part in the world and remains "like water in water." The element in which the subject has a part – the world, an animal, a plant – is not subordinated to it (likewise, the subject cannot be subordinated, in an immediate sense, to the element with which it shares). But the tool is subordinated to the man who uses it, who can modify it as he pleases, in view of a particular result.

The tool has no value in itself – like the subject, or the world, or the elements that are of the same nature as the subject or the world – but only in relation to an anticipated result. The time spent in making it directly establishes its utility, its subordination to the one who uses it with an end in view, and its subordination to this end; at the same time it establishes the clear distinction between the end and the means and it does so in the very terms that its appearance has defined. Unfortunately the end is thus given in terms of the means, in terms of utility. This is one of the most remarkable and most fateful aberrations of language. The purpose of a tool's use always has the same meaning as the tool's use: a utility is assigned to it in turn and so on. The stick digs the ground in order to ensure the growth of a plant; the plant is cultivated in order to be eaten; it is eaten in order to maintain the life of the one who cultivates it. . . . The absurdity of an endless deferral only justifies the equivalent absurdity of a true end, which would serve no purpose. What a "true end" reintroduces is the continuous being, lost in the world like water is lost in water: or else, if it were a being as distinct as a tool, its meaning would have to be sought on the plane of utility, of the tool; it would no longer be a "true end." Only a world in which the beings are indiscriminately lost is superfluous, serves no purpose, has nothing to do, and means nothing: it only has a value in itself, not with a view to something else, this other thing for still another and so on.

The object, on the contrary, has a meaning that breaks the undifferentiated continuity, that stands opposed to immanence or to the flow of all that is – which it transcends. It is strictly alien to the subject, to the self still immersed in immanence. It is the subject's property, the subject's thing, but is nonetheless impervious to the subject.

The perfect – complete, clear and distinct – knowledge that the subject has of the object is entirely external; it results from manufacture;* I know what the object I

---

*As one can see, I have placed the tool and the manufactured object on the same plane, the reason being that the tool is first of all a manufactured object and, conversely, a manufactured object is in a certain sense a tool. The only means of freeing the manufactured object from the servility of the tool is art, understood as a true end. But art itself does not as a rule prevent the object it embellishes from being used for

29

have made is; I can make another one like it, but I would not be able to make another being like me in the way that a watchmaker makes a watch (or that a man in the "age of the reindeer" made a blade of sharp stone), and as a matter of fact I don't know what the being is that I am, nor do I know what the world is and I would not be able to produce another one by any means.

This external knowledge is perhaps superficial, but it alone is capable of reducing man's distance from the objects that it determines. It makes of these objects, although they remain closed to us, that which is nearest and most familiar to us.

The Positing of Immanent Elements in the Sphere of Objects

The positing of the object known clearly and distinctly from without generally defines a sphere of objects, a world, a plane on which it is possible to situate clearly and distinctly, at least so it appears, that which in theory cannot be known in the same way. Thus, having determined stable and simple things which it is possible to make, men situated on the same plane where the things

---

this or that: a house, a table, or a garment are no less useful than a hammer. Few indeed are the objects that have the virtue of serving no function in the cycle of useful activity.

appeared (as if they were comparable to the digging stick, or the chipped stone) elements that were and nonetheless remained continuous with the world, such as animals, plants, other men, and finally, the subject determining itself. This means in other words that we do not know ourselves distinctly and clearly until the day we see ourselves from the outside as another. Moreover, this will depend on our first having distinguished the other on the plane where manufactured things have appeared to us distinctly.

This bringing of elements of the same nature as the subject, or the subject itself, onto the plane of objects is always precarious, uncertain, and unevenly realized. But this relative precariousness matters less than the decisive possibility of a viewpoint from which the immanent elements are perceived from the outside as objects. In the end, we perceive each appearance – subject (ourselves), animal, mind, world – from within and from without at the same time, both as continuity, with respect to ourselves, and as object.*

Language defines, from one plane to the other, the category of subject–object, of the subject considered objectively, clearly and distinctly known from the outside

*Ourselves: what existential philosophy calls, after Hegel, for itself; the object is termed, in the same vocabulary, in itself.

31

insofar as this is possible. But an objectivity of this nature, clear as to the separate positing of one element, remains confused: that element keeps all the attributes of a subject and an object at the same time. The transcendence of the tool and the creative faculty connected with its use are confusedly attributed to the animal, the plant, the meteor; they are also attributed to the entire world.*

The Positing of Things as Subjects

This first confusion being established, a plane of subjects–objects being defined, the tool itself can be placed on it if need be. The object that the tool is can itself be regarded as a subject-object. It then receives the attributes of the subject and takes its place next to those animals, those plants, those meteors, or those men that the object's transcendence, ascribed to them, withdraws from the *continuum*. It becomes continuous with respect to the world

---

*This last muddle is probably the most curious one. If I try to grasp what my thought is designating at the moment when it takes the world as its object, once the absurdity of the world as a separate object, as a *thing* analogous to the manufactured-manufacturing tool, has been foiled, this world remains in me as that continuity from inside to outside, from outside to inside, which I have finally had to discover: I cannot in fact ascribe to subjectivity the limit of myself or of human selves; I cannot limit it in any way.

32

as a whole but it remains separate as it was in the mind of the one who made it: at the moment that suits him, a man can regard this object, an arrow say, as his fellow being, without taking away the operative power and transcendence of the arrow. One could even say that an object thus transposed is not different, in the imagination of the one who conceives it, from what he himself is: this arrow, in his eyes, is capable of acting, thinking, and speaking like him.

The Supreme Being

If we now picture men conceiving the world in the light of an existence that is continuous (in relation to their intimacy, their deep subjectivity), we must also perceive the need for them to attribute to it the virtues of a *thing* "capable of acting, thinking, and speaking" (just as men do). In this reduction to a *thing,* the world is given both the form of isolated individuality and creative power. But this personally distinct power has at the same time the *divine* character of a personal, indistinct, and immanent existence.

In a sense, the world is still, in a fundamental way, immanence without a clear limit (an indistinct flow of being into being – one thinks of the unstable presence of water in water). So the positing, in the world, of a "supreme being," distinct and limited like a thing, is first of

33

all an impoverishment. There is doubtless, in the invention of a supreme being, a determination to define a value that is greater than any other. But this desire to increase results in a diminution. The objective personality of the supreme being situates it in the world next to other personal beings of the same nature, subjects and objects at the same time, like it, but from which it is clearly distinct. Men, animals, plants, heavenly bodies, meteors. . . . If these are at the same time things and intimate beings, they can be envisaged *next to* a supreme being of this type, which, like the others, is in the world, is discontinuous like the others. There is no ultimate equality between them. By definition, the supreme being has the highest rank. But all are of the same kind, in which immanence and personality are mingled; all can be *divine* and endowed with an operative power; all can speak the language of man. Thus, in spite of everything, they basically line up on a plane of equality.

I am obliged to emphasize this aspect of unintentional impoverishment and limitation: nowadays Christians do not hesitate to recognize in the various "supreme beings" of which "primitives" have kept some memory, a first consciousness of the God they believe in, but this nascent consciousness was not a blossoming forth; on the contrary, it was a kind of weakening of an animal sense without compensation.

34

The Sacred

All peoples have doubtless conceived this supreme being, but the operation seems to have failed everywhere. The supreme being apparently did not have any prestige comparable to that which the God of the Jews, and later that of the Christians, was to obtain. As if the operation had taken place at a time when the sense of continuity was too strong, as if the animal or divine continuity of living beings with the world had at first seemed limited, impoverished by a first clumsy attempt at a reduction to an objective individuality. There is every indication that the first men were closer than we are to the animal world; they distinguished the animal from themselves perhaps, but not without a feeling of doubt mixed with terror and longing. The sense of continuity that we must attribute to animals no longer impressed itself on the mind unequivocally (the positing of distinct objects was in fact its negation). But it had derived a new significance from the contrast it formed to the world of things. This continuity, which for the animal could not be distinguished from anything else, which was in it and for it the only possible mode of being, offered man all the fascination of the sacred world, as against the poverty of the profane tool (of the discontinuous object).

The sense of the sacred obviously is not that of the animal lost in the mists of continuity where nothing is

35

distinct. In the first place, while it is true that the confusion has not ceased in the world of mists, the latter do oppose an opaque aggregate to a clear world. This aggregate appears distinctly at the boundary of that which is clear: it is at least distinguishable, externally, from that which is clear. Moreover, the animal accepted the immanence that submerged it without apparent protest, whereas man feels a kind of impotent horror in the sense of the sacred. This horror is ambiguous. Undoubtedly, what is sacred attracts and possesses an incomparable value, but at the same time it appears vertiginously dangerous for that clear and profane world where mankind situates its privileged domain.

The Spirits and the Gods

The equality and inequality of these various existences, all opposed to the *things* that pure objects are, resolves into a hierarchy of *spirits*. Men and the supreme being, but also, in a first representation, animals, plants, meteors . . . are spirits. A scale is built into this conception: the supreme being is in a sense a pure spirit; similarly, the spirit of a dead man does not depend on a clear material reality like that of a living one; finally, the connection of the animal or plant spirit (or the like) with an individual animal or plant is very vague: such spirits are mythical – independent of the given realities. Under these conditions, the hierarchy of spirits tends to be based on a fundamental distinction between spirits that depend on a body, like those of men, and the autonomous spirits of the supreme being, of animals, of dead people, and so on, which tend to form a homogeneous world, a mythical world, within which the hierarchical differences are usually slight. The supreme being, the sovereign deity, the god of heaven, is generally only a more powerful god of the same nature as the others.

The gods are simply mythical spirits, without any substratum of reality. The spirit that is not subordinated to the reality of a mortal body is a god, is purely *divine* (sacred). Insofar as he is himself a spirit, man is divine (sacred), but he is not supremely so, since he is real.

The Positing of the World of Things and of the Body as a Thing

With the positing of a thing, an object, a tool, an implement, or of a domain of objects (where the various coequals of the subject itself assume an objective value), the world in which men move about is still, in a fundamental way, a continuity from the subject's point of view. But the unreal world of sovereign spirits or gods establishes reality, which it is not, as its contrary. The reality of a profane world, of a world of things and bodies, is established opposite a holy and mythical world.

37

Within the limits of continuity, everything is spiritual; there is no opposition of the mind and the body. But the positing of a world of mythical spirits and the supreme value it receives are naturally linked to the definition of the mortal body as being opposed to the mind. The difference between the mind and the body is by no means the same as that between continuity (immanence) and the object. In the first immanence, no difference is possible before the positing of the manufactured tool. Likewise, with the positing of the subject on the plane of objects (of the subject-object), the mind is not yet distinct from the body. Only starting from the mythical representation of autonomous spirits does the body find itself on the side of things, insofar as it is not present in sovereign spirits. The real world remains as a residuum of the birth of the divine world: real animals and plants separated from their spiritual truth slowly rejoin the empty objectivity of tools; the mortal body is gradually assimilated to the mass of things. Insofar as it is spirit, the human reality is holy, but it is profane insofar as it is real. Animals, plants, tools, and other controllable things form a real world with the bodies that control them, a world subject to and traversed by divine forces, but fallen.

The Eaten Animal, the Corpse, and the Thing

The definition of the animal as a thing has become a basic human given. The animal has lost its status as man's fellow creature, and man, perceiving the animality in himself, regards it as a defect. There is undoubtedly a measure of falsity in the fact of regarding the animal as a thing. An animal exists for itself and in order to be a thing it must be dead or domesticated. Thus the eaten animal can be posited as an object only provided it is eaten dead. Indeed it is fully a thing only in a roasted, grilled, or boiled form. Moreover, the preparation of meat is not primarily connected with a gastronomical pursuit: before that it has to do with the fact that man does not eat anything before he has made an object of it. At least in ordinary circumstances, man is an animal that does not *have a part* in that which he eats. But to kill the animal and alter it as one pleases is not merely to change into a thing that which doubtless was not a thing from the start; it is to define the animal as a thing beforehand. Concerning that which I kill, which I cut up, which I cook, I implicitly affirm that *that* has never been anything but a thing. To cut up, cook, and eat a man is on the contrary abominable. It does no harm to anyone; in fact it is often unreasonable not to do something with man. Yet the study of anatomy ceased to be scandalous only a short time ago. And despite appearances, even hardened materialists are still so religious that in their eyes it is always a crime to make a man into a thing – a roast, a stew. . . . In any case, the human attitude toward the body is formidably complex. Insofar as he is spirit, it is man's misfortune to have the body of an animal and thus to be like a thing, but it is the glory of the human body to be the substratum of a spirit. And the spirit is so closely linked to the body as a thing that the body never ceases to be haunted, is never a thing except virtually, so much so that if death reduces it to the condition of a thing, the spirit is more present than ever: the body that has betrayed it reveals it more clearly than when it served it. In a sense the corpse is the most complete affirmation of the spirit. What death's definitive impotence and absence reveals is the very essence of the spirit, just as the scream of the one that is killed is the supreme affirmation of life. Conversely, man's corpse reveals the complete reduction of the animal body, and therefore the living animal, to thinghood. In theory the body is a strictly subordinate element, which is of no consequence for itself – a utility of the same nature as canvas, iron, or lumber.

The Worker and the Tool

Generally speaking, the world of things is perceived as a fallen world. It entails the alienation of the one who created it. This is the basic principle: to subordinate is not only to alter the subordinated element but to be altered oneself. The tool changes nature and man at the same time: it subjugates nature to man, who makes and uses it, but it ties man to subjugated nature. Nature becomes man's property but it ceases to be immanent to him. It is his on condition that it is closed to him. If he places the world in his power, this is to the extent that he forgets that he is himself the world: he denies the world but it is himself that he denies. Everything in my power declares that I have compelled that which is equal to me no longer to exist for its own purpose but rather for a purpose that is alien to it. The purpose of a plow is alien to the reality that constitutes it; and with greater reason, the same is true of a grain of wheat or a calf. If I ate the wheat or the calf in an animal way, they would also be diverted from their own purpose, but they would be suddenly destroyed as wheat and as calf. At no time would the wheat and the calf be the *things* that they are from the start. The grain of wheat *is* a unit of agricultural production; the cow is a head of livestock, and the one who cultivates the wheat is a farmer; the one who raises the steer is a stock raiser. Now, during the time when he is cultivating, the farmer's

41

purpose is not his own purpose, and during the time when he is tending the stock, the purpose of the stock raiser is not his own purpose. The agricultural product and the livestock are things, and the farmer or the stock raiser, during the time they are working, are also things. All this is foreign to the immanent immensity, where there are neither separations nor limits. In the degree that he is the immanent immensity, that he is being, that he is *of* the world, man is a stranger for himself. The farmer is not a man: he is the plow of the one who eats the bread. At the limit, the act of the eater himself is already agricultural labor, to which he furnishes the energy.

CHAPTER III

Sacrifice, the Festival, and the

Principles of the Sacred World

The Need That Is Met
by Sacrifice and Its Principle

The first fruits of the harvest or a head of livestock are sacrificed in order to remove the plant and the animal, together with the farmer and the stock raiser, from the world of things.

The principle of sacrifice is destruction, but though it sometimes goes so far as to destroy completely (as in a holocaust), the destruction that sacrifice is intended to bring about is not annihilation. The thing – only the thing – is what sacrifice means to destroy in the victim. Sacrifice destroys an object's real ties of subordination; it draws the victim out of the world of utility and restores it to that of unintelligible caprice. When the offered animal enters the circle in which the priest will immolate it, it passes from the world of things which are closed to

43

man and are *nothing* to him, which he knows from the outside – to the world that is immanent to it, *intimate,* known as the wife is known in sexual consumption (*consumation charnelle*). This assumes that it has ceased to be separated from its own intimacy, as it is in the subordination of labor. The sacrificer's prior separation from the world of things is necessary for the return to *intimacy,* of immanence between man and the world, between the subject and the object. The sacrificer needs the sacrifice in order to separate himself from the world of things and the victim could not be separated from it in turn if the sacrificer was not already separated in advance. The sac-'rificer declares: "*Intimately,* I belong to the sovereign world of the gods and myths, to the world of violent and uncalculated generosity, just as my wife belongs to my desires. I withdraw you, victim, from the world in which you were and could only be reduced to the condition of a thing, having a meaning that was foreign to your intimate nature. I call you back to the *intimacy* of the divine world, of the profound immanence of all that is."

The Unreality of the Divine World

Of course this is a monologue and the victim can neither understand nor reply. Sacrifice essentially turns its back on real relations. If it took them into account, it would go against its own nature, which is precisely the opposite of

44

that world of things on which distinct *reality* is founded. It could not destroy the animal as a thing without denying the animal's objective *reality*. This is what gives the world of sacrifice an appearance of puerile gratuitousness. But one cannot at the same time destroy the values that found reality and accept their limits. The return to immanent intimacy implies a beclouded consciousness: consciousness is tied to the positing of objects as such, grasped directly, apart from a vague perception, beyond the always unreal images of a thinking based on participation.

The Ordinary Association
of Death and Sacrifice

The puerile unconsciousness of sacrifice even goes so far that killing appears as a way of redressing the wrong done to the animal, miserably reduced to the condition of a thing. As a matter of fact, killing in the literal sense is not necessary. But the greatest negation of the real order is the one most favorable to the appearance of the mythical order. Moreover, sacrificial killing resolves the painful antinomy of life and death by means of a reversal. In fact death is nothing in immanence, but because it is nothing, a being is never truly separated from it. Because death has no meaning, because there is no difference between it and life, and there is no fear of it or defense against it, it invades everything without giving rise to any resistance.

Duration ceases to have any value, or it is there only in order to produce the morbid delectation of anguish. On the contrary, the objective and in a sense transcendent (relative to the subject) positing of the world of things has duration as its foundation: no *thing* in fact has a separate existence, has a meaning, unless a subsequent time is posited, in view of which it is constituted as an object. The object is defined as an operative power only if its duration is implicitly understood. If it is destroyed as food or fuel is, the eater or the manufactured object preserves its value in duration; it has a lasting purpose like coal or bread. Future time constitutes this real world to such a degree that death no longer has a place in it. But it is for this very reason that death means everything to it. The weakness (the contradiction) of the world of things is that it imparts an unreal character to death even though man's membership in this world is tied to the positing of the body as a thing insofar as it is mortal.

As a matter of fact, that is a superficial view. What has no place in the world of things, what is unreal in the real world is not exactly death. Death actually discloses the imposture of reality, not only in that the absence of duration gives the lie to it, but above all because death is the great affirmer, the wonder-struck cry of life. The real order does not so much reject the negation of life that is death as it rejects the affirmation of intimate life, whose

46

measureless violence is a danger to the stability of things, an affirmation that is fully revealed only in death. The real order must annul — neutralize — that intimate life and replace it with the thing that the individual is in the society of labor. But it cannot prevent life's disappearance in death from revealing the *invisible* brilliance of life that is not a *thing*. The power of death signifies that this real world can only have a neutral image of life, that life's intimacy does not reveal its dazzling consumption until the moment it gives out. No one knew *it* was there when it was; it was overlooked in favor of real things: death was one real thing among others. But death suddenly shows that the real society was lying. Then it is not the loss of the thing, of the useful member, that is taken into consideration. What the real society has lost is not a member but rather its truth. That intimate life, which had lost the ability to fully reach me, which I regarded primarily as a thing, is fully restored to my sensibility through its absence. Death reveals life in its plenitude and dissolves the real order. Henceforth it matters very little that this real order is the need for the duration of that which no longer exists. When an element escapes its demands, what remains is not an entity that suffers bereavement; all at once that entity, the real order, has completely dissipated. There is no more question of it and what death brings in tears is the useless consumption of the intimate order.

47

It is a naive opinion that links death closely to sorrow. The tears of the living, which respond to its coming, are themselves far from having a meaning opposite to joy. Far from being sorrowful, the tears are the expression of a keen awareness of shared life grasped in its intimacy. It is true that this awareness is never keener than at the moment when absence suddenly replaces presence, as in death or mere separation. And in this case, the consolation (in the strong sense the word has in the "consolations" of the mystics) is in a sense bitterly tied to the fact that it cannot last, but it is precisely the disappearance of duration, and of the neutral behaviors associated with it, that uncovers a ground of things that is dazzlingly bright (in other words, it is clear that the need for duration conceals life from us, and that, only in theory, the impossibility of duration frees us). In other cases the tears respond instead to unexpected triumph, to good fortune that makes us exult, but always madly, far beyond the concern for a future time.

The Consummation of Sacrifice

The power that death generally has illuminates the meaning of sacrifice, which functions like death in that it restores a lost value through a relinquishment of that value. But death is not necessarily linked to it, and the most solemn sacrifice may not be bloody. To sacrifice is

48

not to kill but to relinquish and to give. Killing is only the exhibition of a deep meaning. What is important is to pass from a lasting order, in which all consumption of resources is subordinated to the need for duration, to the violence of an unconditional consumption; what is important is to leave a world of real things, whose reality derives from a long term operation and never resides in the moment – a world that creates and preserves (that creates for the benefit of a lasting reality). Sacrifice is the antithesis of production, which is accomplished with a view to the future; it is consumption that is concerned only with the moment. This is the sense in which it is gift and relinquishment, but what is given cannot be an object of preservation for the receiver: the gift of an offering makes it pass precisely into the world of abrupt consumption.

This is the meaning of "sacrificing to the deity," whose sacred essence is comparable to a fire. To sacrifice is to give as one gives coal to the furnace. But the furnace ordinarily has an undeniable utility, to which the coal is subordinated, whereas in sacrifice the offering is rescued from all utility.

This is so clearly the precise meaning of sacrifice, that one sacrifices *what is useful*; one does not sacrifice luxurious objects. There could be no sacrifice if the offering were destroyed beforehand. Now, depriving the labor of manufacture of its usefulness at the outset, luxury has already *destroyed* that labor; it has dissipated it in vainglory; in the very moment, it has lost it for good. To sacrifice a luxury object would be to sacrifice the same object twice.

But neither could one sacrifice that which was not first withdrawn from immanence, that which, never having belonged to immanence, would not have been secondarily subjugated, domesticated, and reduced to being a thing. Sacrifice is made of objects that could have been spirits, such as animals or plant substances, but that have become things and that need to be restored to the immanence whence they come, to the vague sphere of lost intimacy.

The Individual, Anguish, and Sacrifice

Intimacy cannot be expressed discursively.

The swelling to the bursting point, the malice that breaks out with clenched teeth and weeps; the sinking feeling that doesn't know where it comes from or what it's about; the fear that sings its head off in the dark; the white-eyed pallor, the sweet sadness, the rage and the vomiting . . . are so many evasions.

What is intimate, in the strong sense, is what has the passion of an absence of individuality, the imperceptible sonority of a river, the empty limpidity of the sky: this is

50

still a negative definition, from which the essential is missing.

These statements have the vague quality of inaccessible distances, but on the other hand articulated definitions substitute the tree for the forest, the distinct articulation for that which is articulated.

I will resort to articulation nevertheless.

Paradoxically, intimacy is violence, and it is destruction, because it is not compatible with the positing of the separate individual. If one describes the individual in the operation of sacrifice, he is defined by anguish. But if sacrifice is distressing, the reason is that the individual takes part in it. The individual identifies with the victim in the sudden movement that restores it to immanence (to intimacy), but the assimilation that is linked to the return to immanence is nonetheless based on the fact that the victim is the thing, just as the sacrificer is the individual. The separate individual is of the same nature as the thing, or rather the anxiousness to remain personally alive that establishes the person's individuality is linked to the integration of existence into the world of things. To put it differently, work and the fear of dying are interdependent; the former implies the thing and vice versa. In fact it is not even necessary to work in order to be the *thing* of fear: man is an individual to the extent that his apprehension ties him to the results of labor. But man is not,

51

as one might think, a thing because he is afraid. He would have no anguish if he were not the individual (the thing), and it is essentially the fact of being an individual that fuels his anguish. It is in order to satisfy the demands of the thing, it is insofar as the world of things has posited his duration as the basic condition of his worth, that he learns anguish. He is afraid of death as soon as he enters the system of projects that is the order of things. Death disturbs the order of things and the order of things holds us. Man is afraid of the intimate order that is not reconcilable with the order of things. Otherwise there would be no sacrifice, and there would be no mankind either. The intimate order would not reveal itself in the destruction and the sacred anguish of the individual. Because man is not squarely within that order, but only partakes of it through a thing that is threatened in its nature (in the projects that constitute it), intimacy, in the trembling of the individual, is holy, sacred, and suffused with anguish.

The Festival

The sacred is that prodigious effervescence of life that, for the sake of duration, the order of things holds in check, and that this holding changes into a breaking loose, that is, into violence. It constantly threatens to break the dikes, to confront productive activity with the precipitate and contagious movement of a purely glorious consumption. The sacred is exactly comparable to the flame that destroys the wood by consuming it. It is that opposite of a thing which an unlimited fire is; it spreads, it radiates heat and light, it suddenly inflames and blinds in turn. Sacrifice burns like the sun that slowly dies of the prodigious radiation whose brilliance our eyes cannot bear, but it is never isolated and, in a world of individuals, it calls for the general negation of individuals as such.

The divine world is contagious and its contagion is dangerous. In theory, what is started in the operation of sacrifice is like the action of lightning: in theory there is no limit to the conflagration. It favors human life and not animality; the resistance to immanence is what regulates its resurgence, so poignant in tears and so strong in the unavowable pleasure of anguish. But if man surrendered unreservedly to immanence, he would fall short of humanity; he would achieve it only to lose it and eventually life would return to the unconscious intimacy of animals. The constant problem posed by the impossibility of being human without being a thing and of escaping the limits of things without returning to animal slumber receives the limited solution of the festival.

The initial movement of the festival is given in elementary humanity, but it reaches the plenitude of an effusion only if the anguished concentration of sacrifice

53

sets it loose. The festival assembles men whom the consumption of the contagious offering (communion) opens up to a conflagration, but one that is limited by a countervailing prudence: there is an aspiration for destruction that breaks out in the festival, but there is a conservative prudence that regulates and limits it. On the one hand, all the possibilities of consumption are brought together: dance and poetry, music and the different arts contribute to making the festival the place and the time of a spectacular letting loose. But consciousness, awake in anguish, is disposed, in a reversal commanded by an inability to go along with the letting loose, to subordinate it to the need that the order of things has – being fettered by nature and self-paralyzed – to receive an impetus from the outside. Thus the letting loose of the festival is finally, if not fettered, then at least confined to the limits of a reality of which it is the negation. The festival is tolerated to the extent that it reserves the necessities of the profane world.

Limitation, the Utilitarian Interpretation of the Festival, and the Positing of the Group

The festival is the fusion of human life. For the thing and the individual, it is the crucible where distinctions melt in the intense heat of intimate life. But its intimacy is dissolved in the real and individualized positing of the ensemble that is at stake in the rituals. For the sake of a *real* community, of a social fact that is given as a thing – of a common operation in view of a future time – the festival is limited: it is itself integrated as a link in the concatenation of useful works. As drunkenness, chaos, sexual orgy, that which it tends to be, it drowns everything in immanence in a sense; it then even exceeds the limits of the hybrid world of spirits, but its ritual movements slip into the world of immanence only through the mediation of spirits. To the spirits borne by the festival, to whom the sacrifice is offered, and to whose intimacy the victims are restored, an operative power is attributed in the same way it is attributed to things. In the end the festival itself is viewed as an operation and its effectiveness is not questioned. The possibility of producing, of fecundating the fields and the herds is given to rites whose least servile operative forms are aimed, through a concession, at cutting the losses from the dreadful violence of the divine world. In any case, positively in fecundation, negatively in propitiation, the community first appears in the festival as a thing, a definite individualization and a shared project with a view to duration. The festival is not a true return to immanence but rather an amicable reconciliation, full of anguish, between the incompatible necessities.

Of course the community in the festival is not posited simply as an object, but more generally as a spirit (as a subject-object), but its positing has the value of a limit to the immanence of the festival and, for this reason, the thing aspect is accentuated. If the festival is not yet, or no longer, under way, the community link to the festival is given in operative forms, whose chief ends are the products of labor, the crops, and the herds. There is no clear *consciousness* of what the festival *actually* is (of what it is at the moment of its letting loose) and the festival is not situated distinctly in consciousness except as it is integrated into the duration of the community. This is what the festival (incendiary sacrifice and the outbreak of fire) is consciously (subordinated to that duration of the common thing, which prevents it from enduring), but this shows the festival's peculiar impossibility and man's limit, tied as he is to clear consciousness. So it is not humanity — insofar as clear consciousness rightly opposes it to animality — restored to immanence. The virtue of the festival is not integrated into its nature and conversely the letting loose of the festival has been possible only because of this powerlessness of consciousness to take it for what it is. The basic problem of religion is given in this fatal misunderstanding of sacrifice. Man is the being that has lost, and even rejected, that which he obscurely is, a vague intimacy. Consciousness could not have become clear in the course of time if it had not turned away from its awkward contents, but clear consciousness is itself looking for what it has itself lost, and what it must lose again as it draws near to it. Of course what it has lost is not outside it; consciousness turns away from the obscure intimacy of consciousness itself. Religion, whose essence is the search for lost intimacy, comes down to the effort of clear consciousness which wants to be a complete self-consciousness: but this effort is futile, since consciousness of intimacy is possible only at a level where consciousness is no longer an operation whose outcome implies duration, that is, at the level where clarity, which is the effect of the operation, is no longer given.

War: The Illusions of the Unleashing of Violence to the Outside

A society's individuality, which the fusion of the festival dissolves, is defined first of all in terms of real works – of agrarian production – that integrate sacrifice into the world of things. But the unity of a group thus has the ability to direct destructive violence to the outside.

As a matter of fact, external violence is antithetical to sacrifice or the festival, whose violence works havoc within. Only religion ensures a consumption that destroys the very substance of those whom it moves. Armed action destroys others or the wealth of others. It can be exerted individually, within a group, but the constituted group

57

can bring it to bear on the outside and it is then that it begins to develop its consequences.

In deadly battles, in massacres and pillages, it has a meaning akin to that of festivals, in that the enemy is not treated as a thing. But war is not limited to these explosive forces and, within these very limits, it is not a slow action as sacrifice is, conducted with a view to a return to lost intimacy. It is a disorderly eruption whose external direction robs the warrior of the intimacy he attains. And if it is true that warfare tends in its own way to dissolve the individual through a negative wagering of the value of his own life, it cannot help but enhance his value in the course of time by making the surviving individual the beneficiary of the wager.

War determines the development of the individual beyond the individual-as-thing in the glorious individuality of the warrior. The glorious individual introduces, through a first negation of individuality, the divine order into the category of the individual (which expresses the order of things in a basic way). He has the contradictory will to make the negation of duration durable. Thus his strength is in part a strength to lie. War represents a bold advance, but it is the crudest kind of advance: one needs as much naïveté – or stupidity – as strength to be indifferent to that which one overvalues and to take pride in having deemed oneself of no value.

58

From the Unfettered Violence of Wars to the Fettering of Man-as-Commodity

This false and superficial character has serious consequences. War is not limited to forms of uncalculated havoc. Although he remains dimly aware of a calling that rules out the self-seeking behavior of work, the warrior reduces his fellow men to servitude. He thus subordinates violence to the most complete reduction of mankind to the order of things. Doubtless the warrior is not the initiator of the reduction. The operation that makes the slave a thing presupposed the prior institution of work. But the free worker was a thing voluntarily and for a given time. Only the slave, whom the military order has made a commodity, draws out the complete consequences of the reduction. (Indeed, it is necessary to specify that without slavery the world of things would not have achieved its plenitude.) Thus the crude unconsciousness of the warrior mainly works in favor of a predominance of the real order. The sacred prestige he arrogates to himself is the false pretense of a world brought down to the weight of utility. The warrior's nobility is like a prostitute's smile, the truth of which is self-interest.

Human Sacrifice

The sacrifices of slaves illustrate the principle according to which *what is useful* is destined for sacrifice. Sacrifice

59

surrenders the slave, whose servitude accentuates the degradation of the human order, to the baleful intimacy of unfettered violence.

In general, human sacrifice is the acute stage of a dispute setting the movement of a measureless violence against the real order and duration. It is the most radical contestation of the primacy of utility. It is at the same time the highest degree of an unleashing of internal violence. The society in which this sacrifice rages mainly affirms the rejection of a disequilibrium of the two violences. He who unleashes his forces of destruction on the outside cannot be sparing of his resources. If he reduces the enemy to slavery, he must, in a spectacular fashion, make a glorious use of this new source of wealth. He must partly destroy these things that serve him, for there is nothing useful around him that can fail to satisfy, first of all, the mythical order's demand for consumption. Thus a continual surpassing toward destruction denies, at the same time that it affirms, the individual status of the group.

But this demand for consumption is brought to bear on the slave insofar as the latter is *his* property and *his* thing. It should not be confused with the movements of violence that have the outside, the enemy, as their object. In this respect the sacrifice of a slave is far from being pure. In a sense it is an extension of military combat, and internal violence, the essence of sacrifice, is not satisfied by it. Intense consumption requires victims at the top who are not only the useful wealth of a people, but this people itself; or at least, elements that signify it and that will be destined for sacrifice, this time not owing to an alienation from the sacred world – a fall – but, quite the contrary, owing to an exceptional proximity, such as the sovereign or the children (whose killing finally realizes the performance of a sacrifice twice over).

One could not go further in the desire to consume the life substance. Indeed, one could not go more recklessly than this. Such an intense movement of consumption responds to a movement of malaise by creating a greater malaise. It is not the apogee of a religious system, but rather the moment when it condemns itself: when the old forms have lost part of their virtue, it can maintain itself only through excesses, through innovations that are too onerous. Numerous signs indicate that these cruel demands were not easily tolerated. Trickery replaced the king with a slave on whom a temporary royalty was conferred. The primacy of consumption could not resist that of military force.

The Military O

From a Balance of Resources a
Expenditures to the Accumul
Forces with a View to Their Gi

Human sacrifice testifies at the same ti
wealth and to a very painful way of spe
ally led to the condemnation of the rath
tems whose growth was slight and in w
ture was commensurate with the resou

The military order put an end to the
responded to an orgy of consumption
rational use of forces for the constant in
The methodical spirit of conquest is cont
of sacrifice and the military kings rejecte
the beginning. The principle of militar
methodical diversion of violence to the
lence rages within, it opposes that violenc
it can. And it subordinates the diversion t

65

does so in a general way. Thus the military order is contrary to the forms of spectacular violence that correspond more to an unbridled explosion of fury than to the rational calculation of effectiveness. It no longer aims at the greatest expenditure of forces, as an archaic social system did in warfare and festivals. The expenditure of forces continues, but it is subjected to a principle of maximum yield: if the forces are spent, it is with a view to the acquisition of greater forces. Archaic society confined itself in warfare to the rounding up of slaves. In keeping with its principles, it could compensate for these acquisitions by means of ritual slaughters. The military order organizes the yield of wars into slaves, that of slaves into labor. It makes conquest a methodical operation, for the growth of an empire.

Positing of an Empire as the Universal Thing

The empire submits from the start to the primacy of the real order. It posits itself essentially as a thing. It subordinates itself to ends that it affirms: it is the administration of reason. But it could never allow another empire to exist at its frontier as an equal. Every presence around it is ordered relative to it in a project of conquest. In this way it loses the simple individualized character of the limited community. It is not a thing in the sense in which

---

PART TWO

Religion Within the Limits of Reason

From the Military Order to Industrial Growth

things fit into the order that belongs to them; it is itself the order of things and it is a universal thing. At this level, the thing that cannot have a sovereign character cannot have a subordinate character either, since in theory it is an operation developed to the limit of its possibilities. At the limit, it is no longer a thing, in that it bears within it, beyond its intangible qualities, an opening to all that is possible. But in itself this opening is a void. It is only the thing at the moment when it is undone, revealing the impossibility of infinite subordination. But it consumes itself in a sovereign way. For essentially it is always a thing, and the movement of consumption must come to it from the outside.

Law and Morality

The empire, being the universal thing (whose universality reveals the void), insofar as its essence is a diversion of violence to the outside, necessarily develops the law that ensures the stability of the order of things. In fact, law gives the attacks against it the sanction of an external violence.

Law defines obligatory relations of each thing (or of each individual-as-thing) with others and guarantees them by the sanction of public force. But here law is only a doublet of the morality that guarantees the same relations by the sanction of an internal violence of the individual.

67

Law and morality also have their place in the empire in that they define a *universal* necessity of the relation of each thing with the others. But the power of morality remains foreign to the system based on external violence. Morality only touches this system at the border where law is integrated. And the connection of the one and the other is the middle term by which one goes from the empire to the outside, from the outside to the empire.

Dualism and Morality

The Positing of Dualism and the Shifting of the Borders of the Sacred and the Profane

In a world dominated by the military order, moving toward universal empire from the start, consciousness is distinctly determined in the measured reflection of the world of things. And this autonomous determination of consciousness brings about, in *dualism,* a profound alteration in the representation of the world.

Originally, within the divine world, the beneficent and pure elements opposed the malefic and impure elements, and both types appeared equally distant from the profane. But if one considers a dominant movement of reflective thought, the divine appears linked to purity, the profane to impurity. In this way a shift is effected starting from the premise that divine immanence is dangerous, that what is sacred is malefic first of all, and destroys through

contagion that which it comes close to, that the beneficent spirits are mediators between the profane world and
the unleashing of divine forces – and seem less sacred in
comparison with the dark deities.

This early shift sets the stage for a decisive change.
Reflective thought defines moral rules; it prescribes universally obligatory relations between individuals and society or between individuals themselves. These obligatory
relations are essentially those that ensure the order of
things. They sometimes take up prohibitions that were
established by the intimate order (such as the one for-
bidding murder). But morality chooses from among the
rules of the intimate order. It sets aside, or at least does
not support, those prohibitions that cannot be granted
universal value, that clearly depend on a capricious liberty
of the mythical order. And even if it gets part of the laws
it decrees from religion, it grounds them, like the others,
in reason; it links them to the order of *things*. Morality lays
down rules that follow universally from the nature of the
profane world, that ensure the duration without which
there can be no operation. It is therefore opposed to the
scale of values of the intimate order, which placed the
highest value on that whose meaning is given in the
moment. It condemns the extreme forms of the ostenta-
tious destruction of wealth (thus human sacrifice, or even
blood sacrifice . . .). It condemns, in a general way, all

useless consumption. But it becomes possible only when sovereignty, in the divine world, shifts from the dark deity to the white, from the malefic deity to the protector of the real order. In fact it presupposes the sanction of the divine order. In granting the operative power of the divine over the real, man had in practice subordinated the divine to the real. He slowly reduced its violence to the sanction of the real order that morality constitutes, provided that the real order conforms, precisely in morality, to the universal order of reason. In reality, reason is the universal form of the thing (identical to itself) and of the operation (of action). Reason and morality united, both resulting from the real order's necessities of preservation and operation, agree with the divine function that exercises a benevolent sovereignty over that order. They rationalize and moralize divinity, in the very movement where morality and reason are divinized.

In this way there appear the elements of the world view that is commonly called dualism and that differs from the first representation, also based on a bipartition, by virtue of a shifting of boundaries and an overturning of values.

In the first representation, the immanent sacred is predicated on the animal intimacy of man and the world, whereas the profane world is predicated on the transcendence of the object, which has no intimacy to which man-

71

kind is immanent. In the manipulation of objects and, generally, in relations with objects, or with subjects regarded as objects, there appear, in forms that are implicit but linked to the profane world, the principles of reason and morality.

The sacred is itself divided: the dark and malefic sacred is opposed to the white and beneficent sacred and the deities that partake of the one or the other are neither rational nor moral.

By contrast, in the dualist evolution the divine becomes rational and moral and relegates the malefic sacred to the sphere of the profane. The world of the spirit (having few connections with the first world of spirits – where the distinct forms of the object were joined to the indistinction of the intimate order) is the intelligible world of the idea, whose unity cannot be broken down. The division into beneficent and malefic is found again in the world of matter, where the tangible form is sometimes apprehensible (in its identity with itself and with its intelligible form, and in its operative power), and other times is not, but remains unstable, dangerous, and not completely intelligible, is only chance, violence, and threatens to destroy the stable and operative forms.

The Negation of the Immanence
of the Divine and Its Positing in the
Transcendence of Reason

The moment of change is given in a passage: the intelligible sphere is revealed in a transport, in a sudden movement of transcendence, where tangible matter is surpassed. The intellect or the concept, situated outside time, is defined as a sovereign order, to which the world of things is subordinated, just as it subordinated the gods of mythology. In this way the intelligible world has the appearance of the divine.

But its transcendence is of a different nature from the inconclusive transcendence of the divine of archaic religion. The divine was initially grasped in terms of intimacy (of violence, of the scream, of being in eruption, blind and unintelligible, of the dark and malefic *sacred*); if it was transcendent, this was in a provisional way, for man who acted in the real order but was ritually restored to the intimate order. This secondary transcendence was profoundly different from that of the intelligible world, which remains *forever* separated from the world of the senses. The transcendence of a more radical dualism is the passage from one world to the other. More exactly, it is the leaving of this world, the leaving of the world, period – for, opposite the sensuous world, the intelligible world

73

is not so much a different world as it is outside the world.

But man of the dualistic conception is opposite to archaic man in that there is no longer any intimacy between him and this world. This world is in fact immanent to him but this is insofar as he is no longer characterized by intimacy, insofar as he is defined by things, and is himself a thing, being a distinctly separate individual. Of course archaic man did not continually participate in the contagious violence of intimacy, but if he was removed from it, the rituals always kept the power to bring him back to it at the proper time. At the level of the dualistic conception, no vestige of the ancient festivals can prevent reflective man, whom reflection constitutes, from being, at the moment of his fulfillment, man of lost intimacy. Doubtless intimacy is not foreign to him; it could not be said that he knows nothing of it, since he has a recollection of it. But this recollection sends him outside a world in which there is nothing that responds to the longing he has for it. In this world even things, on which he brings his reflection to bear, are profoundly separated from him, and the beings themselves are maintained in their incommunicable individuality. This is why for him transcendence does not at all have the value of a separation but rather of a return. No doubt it is inaccessible, being transcendence: in its operation it establishes the impossibility, for the operator, of being immanent to the

74

outcome of the operation. But while the individual that he is cannot leave this world or connect himself with that which goes beyond his own limits, he glimpses in the sudden awakening that which cannot be grasped but which slips away precisely as a *déjà vu*. For him this *déjà vu* is utterly different from that which he sees, which is always separated from him – and for the same reason from itself. It is that which is intelligible to him, which awakens the recollection in him, but which is immediately lost in the invasion of sensory data, which reestablish separation on all sides. This separate being is precisely a *thing* in that it is separated from itself: *it* is the thing and the separation, but *self* is on the contrary an intimacy that is not separated from anything (except that which separates itself from this intimacy, thus *it,* and with it the whole world of separate things).

The Rational Exclusion of the Tangible World and the Violence of Transcendence

A great virtue in the paradox of a transcendence of intimacy results from the complete negation of the *given intimacy* that transcendence is. For the given intimacy is never anything but a contrary of intimacy, because to be given is necessarily to be given in the way that a thing is. It is already to be a thing whose intimacy is necessarily separated from it. The intimacy escapes itself in the movement in which it is given. In fact it is in leaving the world of things that the lost intimacy is regained. But in reality the world of things is not *the world* by itself and pure transcendence toward a pure intelligibility (which is also, glimpsed all at once, in the awakening, a pure unintelligibility) is, within the sensuous world, a destruction at once too complete and impotent.

Doubtless the destruction of the thing in the archaic world had an opposite virtue and impotence. It did not destroy the thing universally by a single operation; it destroyed the thing taken in isolation, *by the negation that is violence,* that is impersonally *in the world.* Now, in its negation the movement of transcendence is no less opposed to violence than it is to the thing that violence destroys. The preceding analysis clearly shows the timidity of that bold advance. It undoubtedly has the same intention as archaic sacrifice, which is, following an ineluctable destiny, at the same time to lift and to preserve the order of things. But if it lifts that order, it is by raising it to the negation of its real effects: the transcendence of reason and morality gives sovereignty, against violence (the contagious havoc of an unleashing), to the sanction of the order of things. Like the operation of sacrifice, it does not condemn, in themselves, the limited unleashings of *de facto* violence, which have rights in the world next to the order of things, but defines them as evil as soon as they place that order in danger.

76

The weakness of sacrifice was that it eventually lost its virtue and finally established an order of sacred *things,* just as servile as that of real objects. The deep affirmation of sacrifice, the affirmation of a dangerous sovereignty of violence, at least tended to maintain an anguish that brought a longing for intimacy to an awakened state, on a level to which violence alone has the force to raise us. But if it is true that an exceptional violence is released in transcendence at the moment of its movement, if it is true that it is the very awakening of possibility – precisely because so complete a violence cannot be maintained for long – the positing of the dualistic awakening has the meaning of an introduction to the somnolence that follows it.

The dualism of transcendence is succeeded by the sleepy positing (which is already given in the initial shifts and which only sleep helps one to tolerate) of the world's division between two principles, both included in this world, of which one is at the same time that of good and the mind, and the other that of evil and matter. Hence there is given, without opposition, an empire of the real order that is a sovereignty of servitude. A world is defined in which free violence has only a negative place.

CHAPTER III

Mediation

The General Weakness of Moral Divinity and the Strength of Evil

Precisely because awakening is the meaning of dualism, the inevitable sleep that follows it reintroduces evil as a major force. The flatness to which a dualism without transcendence is limited opens up the mind to the sovereignty of evil which is the unleashing of violence. The sovereignty of good that is implied by the awakening and realized by the sleep of dualism is also a reduction to the order of things that leaves no opening except toward a return to violence. Dull-minded dualism returns to the position prior to the awakening: the malefic world takes on a value much the same as the one it had in the archaic position. It is less important than it was in the sovereignty of a pure violence, which did not have a sense of evil, but the forces of evil never lost their divine value except within the limits of a developed reflection, and their

79

apparently inferior status cannot prevent ordinary humanity from continuing to live under their power. Several
forms are possible: a cult of execration of a violence considered to be irreducible can capture the interest of a blind
consciousness; and the interest is openly declared if the
execration implies a complete opening to evil, with a view
to a subsequent purification; or evil, evil as such, can reveal
to the confused consciousness that it is worth more to it
than good. But the different forms of the dualistic attitude
never offer anything but a slippery possibility to the mind
(which must always answer at the same time to two ir-
reconcilable demands: lift and preserve the order of
things).

A richer possibility, providing adequate displacements
within its limits, is given in mediation.

The major weakness of dualism is that it offers no
legitimate place for violence except in the moment of
pure transcendence, of rational exclusion of the sensuous
world. But the divinity of the good cannot be maintained
at that degree of purity; indeed, it falls back into the sensuous world. It is the object, on the part of the believer,
of a search for intimate communication, but this thirst for
intimacy will never be quenched. The good is an exclusion of violence and there can be no breaking of the order
of separate things, no intimacy, without violence; the god
of goodness is limited by right to the violence with which

80

he excludes violence, and he is divine, open to intimacy, only insofar as he in fact preserves the old violence within him, which he does not have the rigor to exclude, and to this extent he is not the god of reason, which is the truth of goodness. In theory this involves a weakening of the moral divine in favor of evil.

The Mediation of Evil and the Impotence of the Avenging God

A first mediation of evil has always been possible. If, before my eyes, the real forces of evil kill my friend, the violence introduces intimacy in its most active form. In the state of openness in which I find myself due to a violence undergone, in the mournful revelation of death, I am in accord with the divinity of goodness that condemns a cruel act. In the divine disorder of crime, I call for the violence that will restore the destroyed order. But in reality it is not violence but crime that has opened divine intimacy to me. And, insofar as the vengeance does not become an extension of the irrational violence of the crime, it will quickly close that which crime opened. For only vengeance that is commanded by passion and a taste for untrammeled violence is divine. The restoration of the lawful order is essentially subordinated to profane reality. Thus a first possibility of mediation manifests the exceptionally slippery nature of a god of goodness: he is divine

81

in excluding violence by violence (and he is less so than the excluded violence, which is the necessary mediation of his divinity), but he is divine only insofar as he opposes reason and the good; and if he is a pure rational morality, he owes his remaining divinity to a name, and to a propensity to endure on the part of that which is not destroyed from the outside.

The Sacrifice of the Divinity

In the second form of mediation the violence comes to the divinity from the outside. It is the divinity itself that undergoes it. As in the positing of a god of vengeance, crime is necessary for the return of the intimate order. If there was only man, of the order of things, and the moral divinity, there could not be any deep communication between them. Man included in the order of things would not be able both to lift and to preserve that order. The violence of evil must intervene for the order to be lifted through a destruction, but the offered victim is itself the divinity.

The principle of mediation is given in the sacrifice where the offering is destroyed so as to open a path for the return of the intimate order. But in the mediation of sacrifice the sacrificer's act is not, in theory, opposed to the divine order, the nature of which it extends *imme-diately*. However, the crime that a world of the sovereign

82

good has defined as such is external to the moral divinity. The one who undergoes the violence of evil can also be called the mediator, but this is insofar as he subjects himself to annihilation, insofar as he renounces himself. The ordinary victim of evil, who invoked the god of vengeance, could not receive this name since he had involuntarily undergone the violence of mediation. But the divinity intentionally invokes crime; mediation is the joint accomplishment of violence and of the being that it rends.

In reality the sacrifice of the moral divinity is never the unfathomable mystery that one usually imagines. What is sacrificed is *what serves,* and as soon as sovereignty is reduced to serving the order of things, it can be restored to the divine order only through its destruction, as a thing. This assumes the positing of the divine in a being capable of being really (physically) done away with. The violence thus lifts and preserves the order of things, irrespective of a vengeance that may or may not be pursued. In death the divinity accepts the sovereign truth of an unleashing that overturns the order of things, but it deflects the violence onto itself and thus no longer serves that order: it ceases to be enslaved to it as things themselves are.

In this way it elevates the sovereign good, sovereign reason, above the conservative and operative principles of the world of things. Or rather it makes these intelligible

83

forms that which the movement of transcendence made them: an intelligible beyond of being, *where it situates intimacy.*

But the sacrifice of the divinity is much more closely tied to the general exclusion of the given violences than was transcendence, whose movement of violence was given independently of evil (in reason's being torn away from the sensuous world). The very violence without which the divinity could not have torn itself away from the order of things is rejected as being something that must cease. The divinity remains divine only through that which it condemns.

The Divine Delivered
Over to the Operation

The paradox of a mediation that should not have been does not rest merely on an internal contradiction. In a general way, it controls the contradiction involved in the lifting and maintenance of the real order. Through mediation the real order is subordinated to the search for lost intimacy, but the profound separation between intimacy and things is succeeded by a multiplicity of confusions. Intimacy – salvation – is regarded as a thing characterized by individuality and duration (of the operation). Duration is given to it as a foundation originating in the concern for enduring that is governed by the operation. At the same time it is posited as the result of operations analogous to those of the real order and pursued in that order.

In actual fact the intimate order is subordinated to the real world only in a superficial way. Under the sovereignty of morality, all the operations that claim to ensure the return of the intimate order are those that the real world requires: the extensive prohibitions that are given as the precondition for the return are aimed primarily at preserving the disorder of the world of things. In the end, the man of salvation did more to bring the principles of the order of things into the intimate order than to subordinate that productive order to the destructive consumptions of the intimate order.

So this world of mediation and of works of salvation is led from the start to exceed its limits. Not only are the violences that morality condemns set free on all sides, but a tacit debate is initiated between the works of salvation, which serve the real order, and those works that escape it, that strict morality contests, and that dedicate their useful resources to the sumptuary destructions of architecture, liturgy, and contemplative idleness.

CHAPTER IV

The Rise of Industry

The Positing of a Complete Lack of Relations Between Divine Intimacy and the Real Order

The world of mediation is essentially the world of works. One achieves one's salvation in the same way that one spins wool; that is, one acts, not according to the intimate order, from violent impulses and putting calculations aside, but according to the principles of the world of production, with a view to a future result, which matters more than the satisfaction of desire in the moment. To be exact, nonproductive works do reserve a margin of satisfaction in this world. It is meritorious to introduce a reflection of the divine splendors (that is, of intimacy) here below. Now, besides the merit that is attributed to it, this act has its value in the moment. But seeing that each possibility must be subordinated to the business of salvation, the contradiction between the meritorious act

87

and the divine splendors is even more painful than in the moral work, justified by reason.

The effect of works is eventually to reduce divinity – and the desire for divinity – once again to thinghood. The basic opposition between the divine and the thing, between divine intimacy and the world of the operation, emerges in the negation of the value of works – in the affirmation of a complete absence of relations between divine grace and merits. The negation of the value of works – after the rational exclusion of the sensuous world and the immolation of the divinity – is the third way in which the divine is wrenched away from the order of things. But this admirable refusal makes one think of the fool who jumped into the river to get out of the rain. No doubt the rejection of works is the logical criticism of the compromises of the world of mediation, but it is not a complete criticism. The principle of salvation that reserves the return of lost intimacy for the future and for the world beyond this one misses the essence of the return, which is not only that it can be subordinated to that which it is not, but that it can only be given in the moment – and in the immanence of the here-below. . . . To uphold a salvation deferred to the next world and to repudiate works is to forget that intimacy can be regained only for me – if the two terms are *present* – not intimacy without me. What does restored intimacy mean in itself if it escapes me? Through recollection, the transcendence of reason momentarily rescued thought from the prison of the sensuous world; and the mediation that delivers the divine from the real order introduces the powerlessness of works only because of the absurdity of abandoning the here-below. In any case, one cannot posit divine intimacy unless it is in the particular, without delay, as the possibility of an immanence of the divine *and of man*. But the positing of divine immanence in the negation of the value of works completes the separation of the beyond and the here-below: henceforth the here-below is reduced to thinghood, and the divine order cannot be brought into it – as it was in the monuments and the religious festivities.

It is the most necessary renunciation in one sense: insofar as man ties himself entirely to the real order, insofar as he limits himself to planning operations. But it is not a question of showing the powerlessness of the man of works; it is a question of tearing *man* away from the order of works. And precisely the opposite is accomplished by the negation of their value, which surrenders and confines man to them, changing their meaning. The negation of their value replaces the world of works subordinated to the intimate order with a world in which their sovereignty is consummated, a world of works having no other purpose than its own development. Consequently, production alone is accessible and worthy of

89

interest here-below; the principle of nonproductive destruction is given only in the beyond, and it cannot have any value for the here-below.

General View of the Relations of Production to Nonproductive Destruction

What this negation of the divine value of works makes possible is the reign of autonomous things – in a word, the world of industry. In archaic society, theoretically, the world of things was given as an end for intimate violence, but it could be that end only on one condition: that this violence be considered sovereign, that it be the real end. The concern for production was only an anxious reservation; in reality, *production was subordinated to nonproductive destruction.*

In the military order, the available resources of the world of things were allocated, in principle, to the growth of an empire projecting beyond the closed communities toward the universal.

But military activity only aims to give the order of things, *as it is,* a universal form and value.

So long as the limits of the empire were not reached, production had military force as its primary end, and when these limits were reached, military force was pushed into the background. Moreover, except for what

90

was required for the rational organization of an empire, as concerns the use of the resources produced, in the first phase the order of things maintained ambiguous relations with the archaic society; *production remained subordinated to nonproductive expenditure.*

Once the limit of growth was reached, mediation brought in relations that were just as ambiguous but more complex. Theoretically, the use of production was subordinated to morality, but morality and the divine world were profoundly interdependent. The divine world drew its strength from a violent negation which it condemned, and remained divine in spite of its identification with the real basis of morality, hence with the order of things. Under these conditions the overt contradiction of the archaic world was succeeded by the apparent agreement between a nominal primacy of the divine, consuming production, and, strictly overlapping it, in theory not presenting any difference from it, this no less nominal primacy: the moral order, tied to production. The ambiguity of archaic society continued, but whereas in archaic society the destruction of resources was supposed to favor production owing precisely to its unproductive nature (its divine nature), the society of mediation, claiming salvation as its unproductive end, proposed to achieve that end through productive operations. In this ambiguous perspective, *nonproductive destruction kept a sovereign share, but the principle of the productive operation generally dominated consciousness.*

Consequently, merely by disputing the value of the operation insofar as its effect was supposed to be exerted in the divine order, one arrived at the reign of the autonomous productive operation. Acts ceased to have a subordinate value with regard to rediscovered intimacy (to salvation, or to the bringing of divine splendor into this world). Thus the way was clear for the indefinite development of operative forces. The complete scission between the intimate order and the order of things had the effect of *freeing production* from its archaic purpose (from the nonproductive destruction of its surplus) and from the moral rules of mediation. The excess production could be devoted to the growth of the productive equipment, to capitalist (or postcapitalist) accumulation.

The World of Complete Reduction, or, the Reign of Things

The millenial quest for lost intimacy was abandoned by productive mankind, aware of the futility of the operative ways, but unable to continue searching for that which could not be sought merely by the means it had.

Man began to say: "Let us construct a world whose productive forces grow more and more. We shall meet more and more of our material needs."

92

It soon became apparent that by becoming man of the autonomous thing, man was becoming more estranged from himself than ever before. This complete scission surrendered his life to a movement that he no longer controlled, a movement whose consequences eventually frightened him. Logically this movement engages a large share of production in the installation of new equipment. It has eliminated the possibility of an intense consumption (commensurate with the volume of production) of the excess resources produced: in fact, the products can be delivered only if, in order to obtain the necessary currency, the consumers agree in practice to collaborate in the common project of developing the means of production. This project is what matters and there is nothing preferable to it. There is certainly nothing better that one can do. If one does something, obviously this must be a participation in the project, unless one struggles to make the latter more rational (more effective from the standpoint of development) by revolutionary means. But no one disputes the principle of this sovereignty of servitude.

Indeed, nothing can be opposed to it that might destroy it. For none of the former sovereign entities is able to step forward and sovereignly say: "You will serve me."

The majority of mankind has given its consent to the industrial enterprise, and what presumes to go on existing

93

alongside it gives the impression of a dethroned sovereign. It is clear that the majority of mankind *is right*: compared to the industrial rise, the rest is insignificant. Doubtless this majority has let itself be *reduced to the order of things*. But this generalized reduction, this perfect fulfillment of the thing, is the necessary condition for the conscious and fully developed posing of the problem of man's reduction to thinghood. Only in a world where the thing has reduced everything, where what was once opposed to it reveals the poverty of equivocal positions – and inevitable shifts – can intimacy affirm itself without any more compromises than the thing. Only the gigantic development of the means of production is capable of fully revealing the meaning of production, which is the nonproductive consumption of wealth – the fulfillment of *self-consciousness* in the free outbursts of the intimate order. But the moment when consciousness, reflecting back on itself, reveals itself to itself and sees production destined to be consumed is precisely when the world of production no longer knows what to do with its products.

The Clear Consciousness of Things, or, Science

The condition for achieving clear self-consciousness is science, which is the attainment of a clear consciousness of the real order (i.e., of the world of objects). Science is

94

closely tied to the autonomy of things. And it is itself
nothing but the autonomy of the consciousness of things.
Although consciousness turned away from the intimate
order, which, as far as knowledge goes, is the order of
mythology, it could not be a clear consciousness of
objects so long as it was dependent on mythical determinations. In the first conception, where the tool established the transcendence of the object, it was only in the
confused form of the spirit that consciousness defined its
object. So it was not a clear consciousness of the object
perceived in a separate (transcendent) way: the distinct
consciousness of the object was still not free of the sentiment of self. When attention was focused on sacrifice,
consciousness was at least separated from reflection on
the profane thing, on the intimacy of sacrifice, but it was
then entirely consumed by anguish, obsessed by the feeling of the sacred. Thus the clear consciousness of objects
was given only to the extent that most of the attention
was drawn away from them. The importance of operative
forms and the development of manufacturing techniques
in the movements that were aimed at an imperial (universal) organization brought back a part of the attention to
the world of things. It was when attention was directed
mainly to things that general freedom and the contradiction of judgments became possible. Human thought
escaped the rigid determinations of the mythical order

and got down to the work of science, where objects are clearly and distinctly known. Precise clarity was thus brought into consciousness and it organized the rational modes of consciousness. But as the instrument of knowledge developed, people tried to use it to examine the intimate order. In this way clear consciousness was given a hybrid content. The intimate order, fundamentally *unreal,* adapted its arbitrary mythical representations to the logical forms of the consciousness of objects. It thus introduced into the whole domain of knowledge the sovereign decisions that do not express the intimate order itself but the compromises that enable it to remain intimate while submitting to the principles of the real order. It was only with the complete scission of the intimate and the real, and in the world of the autonomous thing, that science slowly escaped from the hybrid formulations of consciousness. But in its complete success it consummates man's estrangement from himself and realizes, in the case of the scientist, the reduction of all life to the real order. Thus knowledge and activity, developing concurrently without subordinating themselves to one another, finally establish a real, consummate world and humanity, for which the intimate order is represented only through prolonged stammerings. These stammerings still have an uncommon force because they still have the virtue of generally opposing the reality principle with the principle of intimacy, but the good will that receives them is always mixed with disappointment. How meek these voices seem. How defenseless their equivocations leave us, faced with the clear expression of reality. Authority and authenticity are entirely on the side of things, of production and consciousness of the thing produced. All the rest is vanity and confusion.

This unequal situation finally poses the problem in clear terms. The intimate order is not reached if it is not elevated to the authenticity and authority of the real world and real humanity. This implies, as a matter of fact, the replacement of compromises by a bringing of its contents to light in the domain of clear and autonomous consciousness that science has organized. It implies SELF-CONSCIOUSNESS taking up the lamp that science has made to illuminate objects and directing it toward intimacy.

Self-consciousness

The authenticity of a use of science adapted to a knowledge of the intimate order immediately rules out the possibility of giving a learned form to the autonomous declarations of men of intimacy. In the relationship between objective knowledge and intimacy there is doubtless a primary difference: the object can always expect the light that will illuminate it whereas intimacy seeking the light cannot expect it to be projected correctly. If the restoration of the intimate order is to be achieved in the sphere of clear consciousness, which alone has the force to rescue intimacy from equivocations, it still cannot be achieved through a suspension of intimate existence. And insofar as the will to clear consciousness is involved, intimacy will appear to be immediately given in the sphere of distinct knowledge. The difficulty of making distinct knowledge and the intimate order coincide is due to their contrary modes of existence in time. Divine life is immediate, whereas knowledge is an operation that requires suspension and waiting. Answering to the temporal immediacy of the divine life, there was myth and the forms of equivocal thought. And intimate experience can doubtless abandon mysticism, but every time it takes place it must be a complete answer to a total question.

This being true, no one can correctly answer the requirement given in the forms of objective knowledge except by positing a non-knowledge. Irrespective of the fact that the affirmation of a fundamental non-knowledge may be justified on other grounds, the clear consciousness of what is at stake immediately ties divine life to a recognition of its obscure nature, of the night that it opens to discursive knowledge. This immediate coincidence of clear consciousness and the unfettering of the intimate order is not just manifested in the negation of traditional presuppositions; it implies the hypothesis formulated once and for all: "Intimacy is the limit of clear consciousness; clear consciousness cannot clearly and distinctly know anything concerning intimacy, except for the modifications of things that are linked to it." (We don't *know* anything concerning anguish except insofar as it is implied in the fact of the *impossible operation.*) Self-consciousness thus escapes the dilemma of the simultaneous requirement of immediacy and of the operation. The immediate negation diverts the operation toward things and toward the domain of duration.

The weakness of traditional understandings of the intimate order resides in the fact that they have always involved it in the operation; they have either attributed the operative quality to it, or they have sought to attain it by way of the operation. Man placing his essence in the operation obviously cannot bring it about that there is not some link within him between the operation and intimacy. It would be necessary either for intimacy or for the operation to be eliminated. But, being reduced to thinghood by the operation, all that he can do is to undertake the *contrary operation,* a *reduction of the reduction.*

In other words, the weakness of the various religious positions is in having undergone the debasement of the order of things without having tried to modify it. Without exception, the religions of mediation left it as it was,

99

countering it only with the limits of morality. Like the archaic religions, they expressly proposed to maintain it, never lifting it unless they had first ensured its stability. In the end, the reality principle triumphed over intimacy.

What is required by self-consciousness is not really the destruction of the order of things. The intimate order cannot truly destroy the order of things (just as the order of things has never completely destroyed the intimate order). But this real world having reached the apex of its development can be destroyed, in the sense that it can be reduced to intimacy. Strictly speaking, consciousness cannot make intimacy reducible to it, but it can reclaim its own operations, recapitulating them *in reverse,* so that they ultimately cancel out and consciousness itself is strictly reduced to intimacy. Of course this counter operation is not in any way opposed to the movement of consciousness reduced to that which it essentially is – to that which, from the start, each one of us always knew it was. But this will be clear consciousness only in one sense. It will regain intimacy only in darkness. In so doing, it will have reached the highest degree of distinct clarity, but it will so fully realize the possibility of man, or of being, that it will rediscover the night of the animal intimate with the world – *into which it will enter.*

100

The General Destruction of Things

To begin with, we have clear consciousness in its elaborated form. Further, the world of production, the order of things, has reached the point of development where it does not know what to do with its products. The first condition makes destruction possible; the second makes it necessary. But this cannot be done in the empyrean, that is, in unreality, to which the religious approach usually leads. The moment of decision demands, on the contrary, a consideration of the poorest and least intimate aspects of the problem. We must descend now to the lowest level of the world of man's reduction to thinghood.

I can shut myself up in my room, and look there for the clear and distinct meaning of the objects that surround me.

Here is my table, my chair, my bed. They are here as a result of labor. In order to make them and install them in my room it was necessary to forego the interest of the moment. As a matter of fact I myself had to work to pay for them, that is, in theory, I had to compensate for the labor of the workers who made them or transported them, with a piece of labor just as useful as theirs. These products of labor allow me to work and I will be able to pay for the work of the butcher, the baker, and the farmer who will ensure my survival and the continuation of my work.

101

Now I place a large glass of alcohol on my table.

I have been useful. I have bought a table, a glass, etc.

But this table is not a means of labor: it helps me to drink alcohol.

In setting my drinking glass on the table, to that extent *I have destroyed the table,* or at least I have destroyed the labor that was needed to make it.

Of course I have first completely destroyed the labor of the winegrower, whereas my absorption has only destroyed a minute amount of the carpenter's labor. At least this table in this room, heavy with the chains of labor, for a time had no other purpose than my breaking loose.

I am now going to recall the use I have made of the money earned at my work table.

If I have wasted part of that money, wasted part of the time the rest enabled me to live, the destruction of the table is already more advanced. Had I just once seized the moment by the hair, all the preceding time would already be in the power of that moment seized. And all the supplies, all the jobs that allowed me to do so would suddenly be destroyed; like a river, they would drain endlessly into the ocean of that brief instant.

In this world there is no immense undertaking that has any other end than a definitive loss in the futile moment. Just as the world of things is nothing in the

102

superfluous universe where it is dissolved, the mass of efforts is nothing next to the futility of a single moment. The free yet submissive moment, furtively involved in minute operations by the fear of letting oneself *lose time* is what justifies the pejorative value of the word futile.

This introduces, as a basis for *clear self-consciousness,* a consideration of the objects that are dissolved and destroyed in the intimate moment. It is a return to the situation of the animal that eats another animal; it is a negation of the difference between the object and myself or the general destruction of objects as such in the field of consciousness. Insofar as I destroy it in the field of my clear consciousness, this table ceases to form a distinct and opaque screen between the world and me. But this table could not be destroyed in the field of my consciousness if I did not give my destruction its consequences in the real order. The real reduction of the reduction of the real order brings a fundamental reversal into the economic order. If we are to preserve the movement of the economy, we need to determine the point at which the excess production will flow like a river *to the outside.* It is a matter of endlessly consuming – or destroying – the objects that are produced. This could just as well be done without the least *consciousness.* But it is insofar as clear consciousness prevails that the objects actually destroyed

103

will not destroy humanity itself. The destruction of the subject as an individual is in fact implied in the destruction of the object as such, but war is not the inevitable form of the destruction: at any rate, it is not the conscious form (that is, if self-consciousness is to be, in the general sense, human).

To whom . . .

The positing of a religious attitude that would result from clear consciousness, and would exclude, if not the ecstatic form of religion, then at least its mystical form, differs radically from the attempts at fusion that exercise minds anxious to remedy the weakness of current religious positions.

Those in the religious world who are alarmed about the lack of harmony, who look for the link between the different disciplines, who are determined to deny that which opposes the sannyasi to the Roman prelate, or the Sufi to the Kierkegaardian pastor, complete the emasculation – on both sides – of that which already originates in a compromise of the intimate order with the order of things. The spirit farthest removed from the virility necessary for joining *violence and consciousness* is the spirit of "synthesis." The endeavor to sum up that which separate religious possibilities have revealed, and to make their shared content the principle of a human life raised to universality, seems unassailable despite its insipid results, but for anyone *to whom human life is an experience to be carried as far as possible,* the *universal sum* is necessarily that of the religious sensibility in time. Synthesis is most clearly what reveals the need to firmly link this world to that which the religious sensibility is in its universal sum in time. This clear revelation of a decline of the whole living religious world (salient in these synthetic forms that abandon the narrowness of a tradition) was not given so long as the archaic manifestations of religious feeling appeared to us independently of their meaning, like hieroglyphs that could be deciphered only in a formal way; but if that meaning is now given, if, in particular, the behavior of sacrifice, the least clear but the most divine and the most common, ceases to be closed to us, the whole of human experience is restored to us. And if we raise ourselves personally to the highest degree of clear consciousness, it is no longer the servile thing in us, but rather the *sovereign* whose presence in the world, from head to foot, from animality to science and from the archaic tool to the non-sense of poetry, is that of universal humanity. Sovereignty designates the movement of free and internally wrenching violence that animates the whole, dissolves into tears, into ecstasy and into bursts of laughter, and reveals the impossible in laughter, ecstasy, or tears. But the impossible thus revealed is not an equivocal position; it is the sovereign self-consciousness that, precisely, no longer turns away from itself.

TO WHOM LIFE IS AN EXPERIENCE TO BE CARRIED AS
FAR AS POSSIBLE. . . .

I have not meant to express my thought but to
help you clarify what you yourself think. . . .

You are not any more different from me than
your right leg is from your left, but what joins us
is THE SLEEP OF REASON — WHICH PRODUCES MONSTERS.

Appendix

General Table
and References

I feel obliged to present a table* that makes it possible to visualize the successive possibilities as a single develop- ment. This figure emphasizes the dialectical character of the development whose phases go from opposition to opposition and from stagnation to movement. But above all it offers the advantage of being clear.

Unfortunately this clarity has its drawbacks.

It tends to deprive my exposition of a virtue that it must claim.

As far as possible, I have tried to present the foregoing logical movement in the form it would have in the final state of consciousness, that is, detached from an elabora- tion of its historical or ethnographic forms. For this reason, I have excluded discussion of those forms as well as references pertaining to them.

*The editor of Bataille's complete works notes that this table was not found among the author's papers. [trans. note]

I was all the less inclined to link these developments to an analysis of the particular realities as they are distinctly separate from the latter: by definition these realities correspond in a capricious, imperfect way to the necessity they express. In the last instance this necessity may have operated unreservedly without ever having been inevitable at a precise moment. Forms that I have presented as being integral with one another may have developed at times one after the other. Moreover, I have had to articulate the stages of a movement as if there were a discontinuity, whereas continuity is the rule and transitional forms have a considerable place in history. Hybrid forms, resulting from contacts in time of very different civilizations, also introduce confusion. Finally, it is clear that conditions regularly present at a particular stage may reappear and become operative at some subsequent stage.

Of course this apparent casualness does not at all preclude possible, or rather, necessary, discussions. I repeat that this piece of work is far from completion. And in fact the completed work, if it is possible, should result from such discussions. It is a common error of perspective to think that by contesting a particular point one contests the solidity of the outlined whole. This whole is itself the result of my own contestations and not one of them failed to enrich it, although, past a certain point, I did not have to make any substantial changes. Given the general cohesion, a justified contradiction is not the attack that the contradictor easily imagines; it is a help. (I am happy to cite as an example the friendly interventions of Mircea Éliade: it was one of them in particular that enabled me to situate the "supreme being" in the world of spirits.) While it is true that a cohesion must necessarily distance itself from the capricious data of the historical world, there is not one of these data that one should not try to reduce to the whole and only insofar as the whole has been polished by these reductions can it easily reveal to others the contents of their own thought.

I would like to help my fellow beings get used to the idea of an *open* movement of reflection. This movement has nothing to conceal, nothing to fear. It is true that the results of thought are strangely tied to tests of rivalry. No one can entirely separate what he thinks from the real authority the expression of this thought will have. And authority is acquired in the course of games whose traditional, somewhat arbitrary rules oblige the one who expresses himself to give his thought the idea of a flawless and definitive operation. This is an entirely excusable comedy, but it isolates thought in bird-like displays that no longer have anything to do with a real process, necessarily painful and open, always seeking help and never admiration.

119

This justification of the method followed does not prevent me from seeing its real disadvantages, which concern intelligibility. Even if representations do not take on their full meaning until they detach themselves from the realities to which they refer (without being positively grounded in any of them in particular), they will not be fully understandable if they do not in general shed light on the historical forms. This schema, which needed to systematically avoid precise references, was nonetheless to be followed by an elucidation of history with the help of its figures.

I will confine myself, however, to one example chosen with the intention of showing in a general way the freedom that is necessary to this mode of interpretation.

There should be some point in stating here that Islam cannot generally be regarded as a form corresponding to a single one of the definitions given. From the outset Islam was a military order, limiting, even more strictly than others, those activities whose purpose was not force and military conquest. But it presents these peculiarities: it went, suddenly and discontinuously, from a spendthrift archaic civilization to a military one; but it did not realize all the possibilities of the latter, for *at the same time* it experienced, in an abridged form as it were, the development of an economy of salvation. Hence in its first phase it did not have all the characteristics of the military order

120

nor all those of the economy of salvation. In the first place it was not amenable to the autonomous development of clear consciousness or of philosophy (yet, through the iconoclasm that it opposed to the Byzantine hieratism, it went further than the classic military order in reducing the forms of art to reason). Second, it dispensed with mediation and upheld a transcendence of the divine world, which conformed to the military type of a violence directed to the outside. But what is true of early Islam is not at all true of late Islam. *Once the Moslem empire reached its limits of growth,* Islam became a perfect economy of salvation. It merely had forms of mediation that were less pronounced and more pathetic than Christianity. But like Christianity it gave rise to a costly spiritual life. Mysticism and monasticism developed; the arts remained in principle within the limits of iconoclasm but escaped rational simplification in every way. Owing to the relatively small part played by internal violence, Islam was even the most stable of the different economies of salvation, the one that best ensured the stability of a society.

This kind of application of a method aims to show, on the one hand, the distance that separates from reality the figures of a schema, and on the other hand, the possibility of reducing reality after the event.

The references that follow are subject to the same reservation. But like these applications, they should help to situate a construction that is rather oddly disconnected from its foundations. While maintaining the detached character of my statements, it seems possible, or should I say, necessary, *after the event,* to connect them in a general way to some of their origins. I do this in the form of references to writings whose authors in some way moved toward the precise conceptions of this "theory," or whose contents offer reference points that guided my steps.

I will give them in random sequence, following the alphabetical order of the authors' names.

GEORGES DUMÉZIL. *Mitra-Varuna*, Zone Books, 1988. The interpretations of Indo-European mythology that are pursued in the admirable works of Georges Dumézil, especially those found in this volume – after *Ouranos-Varuna* (1931) and *Flamine-Brahmane* (1933) – correspond to the constructions that I have developed: the consciously Hegelian theses, antitheses, and syntheses of Georges Dumézil set forth the opposition of pure violence (on the dark and malefic side of the divine world – Varuna and the Gandharva, Romulus and the Luperci) to the divine order that accords with profane activity (Mitra and the Brahmans, Numa, Dius Fidius and the Flamines), and its resolution in the external and efficacious violence of a human and rational military order.

122

ÉMILE DURKHEIM. *The Elementary Forms of the Religious Life*, Free Press, 1965. Émile Durkheim seems to me to be unjustly disparaged nowadays. I take my distance from his doctrine but not without retaining its essential lessons.

ALEXANDRE KOJÈVE. *Introduction to the Reading of Hegel*, Cornell University Press, 1980. This work is an explication of Hegel's *Phenomenology of the Spirit*. The ideas that I have developed here are substantially present in it. The correspondences between the Hegelian analysis and this "theory of religion" would still need to be specified. The differences between the two representations appear to me to be easily reducible. The main difference concerns the conception that makes the destruction of the subject the condition – necessarily unrealizable – of its adequation to the object. Doubtless this implies from the start a state of mind radically opposed to Hegelian "satisfaction," but here the contraries coincide (they only coincide, and the opposition in which they coincide cannot this time be overcome by any synthesis: there is an identity of the particular being and the universal, and the universal is not truly given except in the mediation of particularity, but the resolution of the individual into the non-individual does not overcome pain [or painful joy] except in death, or in the state of ataraxia – comparable to the death of complete satisfaction; hence the maintenance of the reso-

lution at the level prior to ecstasy, which is not a resolution . . .). Having had to cite the work of Alexandre
Kojève here, I must emphasize one point: whatever opinion one may have of the correctness of his interpretation
of Hegel (and I believe the possible criticisms on this
point should be assigned only a limited value), this *Introduction*, relatively accessible, is not only the primary
instrument of *self-consciousness;* it is the only way to view
the various aspects of human life – the political aspects in
particular – differently from the way a child views the
actions of adults. No one today can claim to be educated
without having assimilated its contents. (I would also like
to underscore the fact that Alexandre Kojève's interpretation does not deviate in any way from Marxism; similarly, it is easy to see that the present "theory" is always
rigorously based on economic analysis.)

SYLVAIN LÉVI. *La doctrine du sacrifice dans les brahmanas*, E.
Leroux, 1898. The interpretation of sacrifice is the foundation of *"self-consciousness."* Sylvain Lévi's work is one of
the essential components of that interpretation.

MARCEL MAUSS. *Sacrifice: Its Nature and Function*, University of Chicago Press, 1969. *The Gift*, Norton, 1967. The
first of these works is the authoritative treatment of the
historical data on ancient sacrifice. The second forms the

basis of any understanding of economy as being tied to forms of destruction of the excess of productive activity.

SIMONE PÉTREMENT. *Le dualisme dans l'histoire de la philosophie et des religions*, Gallimard, 1946. Simone Pétrement, whose moral position is that of the ancient gnostics, presents the question of the history of dualism with a remarkable clarity in this little book. Starting from her data, I have analyzed the transition from archaic dualism to the dualism of spirit/matter, or rather, of transcendence/ sensuous world, the only dualism considered by the author.

BERNARDINO DE SAHAGÚN. *General History of the Things of New Spain*, University of Utah Press, 1974–1982. This Spanish monk's investigation of conditions in Mexico prior to the Conquest, especially his inquiry into the human sacrifices celebrated in great numbers in the temples of Mexico, was conducted using Aztec informants who had been witnesses. It is the most reliable and the most detailed document we have concerning the terrible aspects of sacrifice. We must necessarily reject the representations of man or of religion that leave their extreme forms under the cloak of an alleged monstrousness. Only an image that shines through them measures up to the intimate movements that consciousness turns away from but that it must ultimately return to.

125

R. H. TAWNEY. *Religion and the Rise of Capitalism*, Harcourt, Brace, & Co., 1926. This book's analyses, based on a wealth of information, show the importance of the deliberate disjunction of the sacred and profane worlds that was at the origin of capitalism. Protestantism introduced the possibility of this disjunction by denying the religious value of works: the world of the operative forms of economic activity thus received – but in the course of time – an autonomy that enabled the rapid increase of industrial accumulation.

MAX WEBER. *The Protestant Ethic and the Spirit of Capitalism*, Macmillan, 1977. Max Weber's famous study linked, for the first time in a precise way, the very possibility of accumulation (of the use of wealth for developing the forces of production) to the positing of a divine world that had no conceivable connection with the here-below, where the operative form (calculation, selfishness) radically separates the glorious consumption of wealth from the divine order. More than Tawney, Max Weber dwelled on the decisive change introduced by the Reformation, which made accumulation basically possible by denying the value of works and by condemning nonproductive expenditure.